BITE-SIZED
BOOKS

A Bite-Sized Business Book

The Six Things That All Customers Want

A Practical Guide to Delivering Simply Brilliant Customer Service

Nigel Greenwood

Simply Customer Ltd
www.simplycustomer.co.uk

Published by Bite-Sized Books Ltd 2015

Although the publisher and author have used reasonable care in preparing this book, the information it contains is distributed as is and without warranties of any kind. This book is not intended as legal, financial, social or technical advice and not all recommendations may be suitable for your situation. Professional advisors should be consulted as needed. Neither the publisher nor the author shall be liable for any costs, expenses or damages resulting from use of or reliance on the information contained in this book.

© Copyright Nigel Greenwood 2015

Bite-Sized Books Ltd
Cleeve Croft, Cleeve Road, Goring RG8 9BJ UK
information@bite-sizedbooks.com
Registered in the UK. Company Registration No: 9395379

Contents

Introduction

Most businesses I've worked with think they deliver great customer service – but most of their customers disagree. The problem is that most of the time customer service is OK and you only hear from customers when something goes wrong – most businesses don't do enough to understand what service their customer wants and forget about the small things that make the difference between OK and great.

I wrote this book because I'm passionate about great customer service and because over the last 30 years I've learned how a business of any size can deliver it and seen what fantastic results even small changes can bring. In the book I explain why great service is important and how to deliver it.

It's designed to help large and small businesses whether start-ups or established. Because it covers 30 years' experience, there's a lot in it so it can seem daunting if you try to do everything at once! – that's why I'd suggest you read through it first and then go through one chapter at a time, not moving onto the next chapter until you have made the changes suggested and seen the results for yourself. Most chapters have a checklist at the end to help you, and there are larger versions in the final chapter that you can print out and use. This will help you build a complete picture of how customers see and want to interact with your business and give you a "virtuous circle" of continually improving your service, your sales and ultimately your profits!

I hope you enjoy it and find it useful. It would be great to get your feedback!

Chapter 1

What sort of friend is your business?

It may sound strange thinking of your business as a friend, but I've read lots of books about brand image and customer experience and just ended up confused until I realised that it's really very simple –

Think of your business as a person. It has relationships like any person, only these are with customers. So brand image is all about what sort of person your customers think your business is and customer experience is all about how they expect the business to behave.

For example, take Apple. I think of them as a younger person who is always coming up with new ideas, never sitting still for long. Great as a friend in some ways but you get the feeling that when you are talking to them they aren't really listening, just thinking about the next thing they want to say or do. Some people love them and some hate them. Now, if you think of John Lewis or Marks & Spencer as a person, they are that middle aged friend who is a really good listener, always there when you need them, but they don't often come up with new places to go or things to do.

So think about what type of friend you want your business to be. Once you are clear what type of personality it is, then it is much easier to think about how that type of personality would behave, and that then helps you decide how you will serve your customers.

Once you have decided on your business's personality, it's important to make sure everything your business does reflects that. For example, Amazon's image has been hit recently as we found that they structured their company to avoid paying tax and that they have some harsh working practices. All legal of course, but many people were surprised that a business they saw almost as a friend would behave in what could be viewed as an underhand way.

I know you have lots to think about when starting up or running a business, but THIS IS THE MOST IMPORTANT THING YOU WILL DO. That's because it acts as a blueprint for everything your business does in the future – once you know what type of friend your business is, you will check every new idea, product, process or service to make sure it is what customers would expect. So, before you go any further, take time to describe what personality your business has and how people would expect it to behave:

My business is a:	
It behaves like this:	

Chapter 2

Why it's worth focusing on customer service

Reason 1: Customers will buy more from you more often

The US poet Maya Angelou once said "people will forget what you said, people will forget what you did, but people will never forget how you made them feel". Although she was talking about relationships in general, it is true for businesses. Think about why you are a customer of businesses you regularly use – your favourite restaurant for example and it's probably because the service and food is good, you enjoy the experience and feel you get good value. Research shows that 70% of buying experiences are based on how the customer feels they are being treated.

Reason 2: Customers will stay with you longer

There is a lot of research about why customers stop buying from a business. It shows that customers are 4 times more likely to leave if the problem is service related than if it is price or product related. For example, there is a restaurant near me which serves great food at good prices – but I've only been twice and often drive past it to go to a more expensive restaurant. It's not because I like spending money (after all, I'm from Yorkshire!) but because the service is very poor in the cheaper restaurant and great in the more expensive one so I feel they care much more about me as a customer.

And what's important about keeping customers for longer? – well, on average existing customers will spend twice as much as a new customer would and they are easier to sell to – your chances of selling to an existing customer are typically 60-70% and your chances of selling to a new customer are between 5 to 20%

Reason 3: Most people don't tell you if they aren't satisfied with your service

If you already run a business, you probably think that you already deliver great customer service – a survey by Bain & Co found that 80% of business owners think that. But the same survey found that only 8% of customers think they get great customer service. I can count on my fingers how many businesses I deal with consistently give great service but I'd need a calculator to count how many don't – so I think many businesses are kidding themselves if they think they are great at customer service. Most don't ask for customer feedback anyway, and customers don't normally tell a business if they aren't happy with the service (unless it's really bad!)

For every 100 people that are not satisfied with the service they get, only 4 will tell the company. Think about having a meal in a restaurant – when the manager asks if everything has been OK, how many of us just say yes, even though the service was slow or the food badly cooked, and then walk out vowing never to go back?

Of the 96 that don't complain, 91 will stop using the business at some point in the future so even if you don't get many complaints, you may be about to lose customers without realising it.

Even if you are delivering good service, you can still do more and get better results – customers who rate you 5 out of 5 are 6 times more likely to buy from you again as customers who "only" rate you 4.8 out of 5!

Reason 4: it makes life difficult for your competitors

If you don't focus on service, you will start to lose customers. Many businesses react by competing on price. Look at how Aldi and Lidl took market share from Sainsbury's, Tesco and Morrison's by offering cheaper products. Every supermarket except one reacted by lowering their prices. The one that didn't? Marks & Spencer – they continued to focus on service and didn't lose any market share to competitors.

Reason 5: it's profitable

Research from Deloitte LLP proved that customer centric companies are 60% more profitable than those who don't focus on customer service.

For example – for the first 15 years it existed, Ryanair were known as a cheap, no frills airline who had never worried about customer service, just focusing on price. But their success meant that competitors came in and started to undercut them, meaning they had to react. They started to improve their customer service and, within 18 months, saw a 25% increase in passengers, a 32% increase in profits and a 40% drop in complaints.

So, keeping customers happy by delivering great service is key to profitability. Put simply, happy customers stay longer, complain less and buy more, meaning lower costs and higher income for a business.

Not only that, happy customers are more likely to tell other people about how great you are to deal with, effectively acting as unpaid salespeople for your business – even if they have had cause to complain. A customer who isn't happy will on average tell 9 to 15 people about their experience and advise them not to deal with you. A customer who is happy that their issue has been resolved will tell 4 to 6 people about how great you are to do business with. My daughter Anna started a small online jewellery business. One of her first customers complained that the item had been broken in the post. Anna apologised immediately and sent a replacement plus an extra item as a further apology. The customer was delighted and tweeted her 60,000 followers, telling them what a great business it was. Orders flooded in from around the world!

Chapter 3

Who are your customers anyway?

It's really important for a business to have a clear view of its target market: the type of customer, what products or service they need, what price they are prepared to pay, what distribution and communication channels they use, and what the competition offers. That can be really complicated and it can be hard to get the information you need (sometimes you're not even really sure what questions to ask) – when I set up my business I spent 18 months researching competitors and the target market then planning out how the business would work.

It's much simpler when thinking about customer service – it's about understanding how your customers want to do business with you – what their needs and expectations are and how they want to feel about doing business with you.

It starts with the personality of your business or your brand image – do they expect you to be innovative or traditional, efficient or friendly (or both!), how do they expect you to behave? So if you haven't read Chapter 1 or completed the questionnaire at the end of it yet, go back and do it now!

I've worked with businesses who had dozens of customer segments, but no matter how large your business is, there are only 4 different types of customer to consider when you think about customer service:

1. Potential customers – think about people who haven't yet heard about you. Where would they expect you to promote your business – networking, advertising, online, newspaper adverts, radio. What should you say about your business – they need a reason to consider using you. Remember that 70% of buying decisions are based on how customers think they are treated so promote how customer focused you are and how you make it easy for them to do business with you. Make sure you don't make any promises you can't keep at this point – avoid the risk of letting customers down. I was asked to help a business that was having to hire extra staff just to deal with customer queries and didn't understand why. When I mapped the customer journey

they were promising to send customers information the next day even though they knew they had a backlog and it would take 5 days. They weren't telling customers it would take that long because they didn't want to upset them and risk losing the business – but all that happened was that customers were phoning to chase for the information and getting frustrated because the business hadn't kept its promise. Simply starting to explain to customers that it would take 5 days because there had been more demand than they had expected stopped all the queries, reduced the cost of answering the calls and meant customers were happy.

2. Existing customers – make sure you are easy to do business with, that they can contact you easily in the way they want to. It's also important to give them the information they want when they need it. Try thinking of potential problems for them and solving them before they happen. 18 months after I bought a new TV from a local dealer it developed a fault. I phoned them and they arranged for an engineer from the manufacturer to call the next day. They had also realised that the warranty had expired and had already sorted that out with the manufacturer so I didn't have to pay for the repair! Guess which company I'll buy my next TV from (and I've already referred 3 people to them).

3. Former customers – it might sound strange to think about former customers, but they will still tell other potential customers about your business, and, if you treat them well when they decide not to do business with you again, you increase the chances of them coming back again at some point. Make sure you thank them for their business and that you'll welcome them back at any time – keep in touch with them by sending any information you think may be relevant to them.

4. Staff – most businesses forget to treat staff the way that they treat customers, but it's extremely important. To many customers, your staff are the main part of your business they see – almost like seeing your brand image come to life! Later, I explain

"People will forget what you said, people will forget what you did, but people will never forget how you made them feel." - Maya Angelou

If you think what the customer would expect, for the website it could be location, opening hours, example menu, a phone number to contact and possibly a way to contact by email. If the website didn't have opening times on and the customer had to phone to find out, it isn't easy for them to do business with the café so some may call but many won't even try to visit as it's too much effort. So, from the website, a customer could visit or phone:

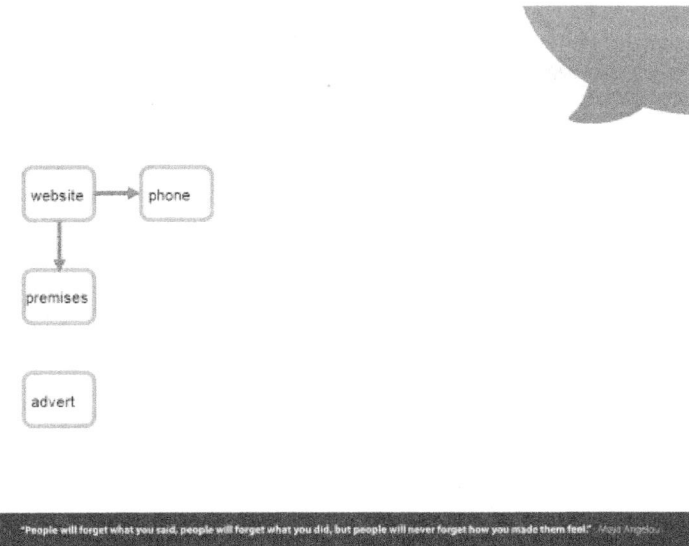

"People will forget what you said, people will forget what you did, but people will never forget how you made them feel." - Maya Angelou

If they phone and there's no answer or answering service they are likely to go somewhere else. When they phone they could book a table or could decide not to go:

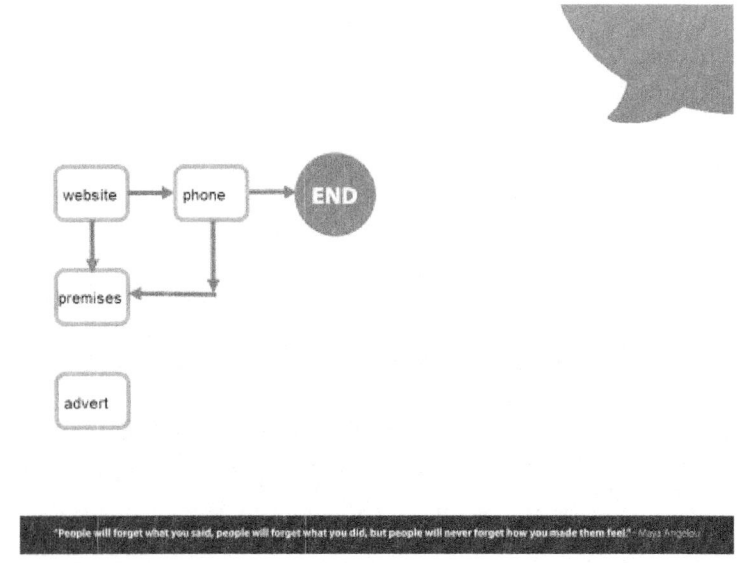

"People will forget what you said, people will forget what you did, but people will never forget how you made them feel." - Maya Angelou

From the advert they could go to the website, phone or visit:

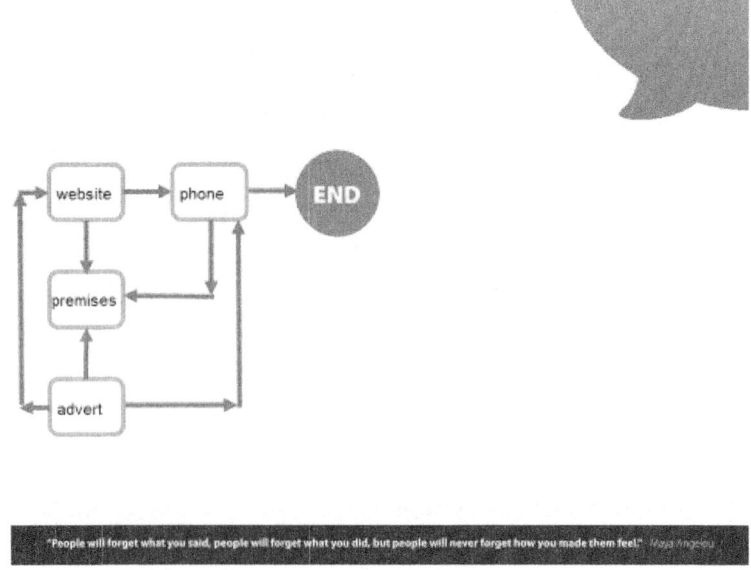

"People will forget what you said, people will forget what you did, but people will never forget how you made them feel." - Maya Angelou

Customer journey mapping is a great way to show all the different touch points that a customer could have with a business, how they interact and what the customer would expect at each point. To start, stick a large piece of paper (flipchart size works well for most businesses) on a wall with the longest sides at the top and bottom. Draw 3 lines down the page, roughly splitting it into 4 sections. The first section is awareness, the second consideration, the third is customer and the final one is leaving.

Under awareness, write down all the different ways someone could become aware of your business such as website, referral, shop, adverts. Under consideration, write down all the different ways someone could get more information about your business and buy your products or services such as website, shop, phone etc. Under customer, think about all the different things a customer could see whilst they are a customer – it could be a leaflet, email, website, shop, phone, personal visit. Finally, under leaving, think about how a customer would tell you they no longer want to do business with you and what they would see once you had been told. It could be they would phone, visit or e-mail you then get a letter or e-mail from you, maybe a final bill and then maybe e-mail newsletters.

To complete the map, take each point you've written down (these are the customer touch points) and draw arrows to where the customer could go next or what they would see next. For example, someone may see one of your adverts and could go to your website, visit your shop or phone you. As you map each possible journey, think about how easy or difficult it is for a customer to do what they want to do and start to list what the customer issues may be and how you could make it easier for them.

When you've done your map, use the touch points on the map for your customer feedback:

When you know what the touch points are, you can ask your customers about each one. In the above example, you may choose to ask: when you visited our website, was there all the information you needed? Was it easy to use?

There are 3 simple ways to get customer feedback

1. Ask your staff what customers are saying – they are the people who talk to customers all the time. Asking them what customers are happy and unhappy about not only gives you an up to the minute view but also motivates your staff as they feel involved and valued.

2. Ask your customers – this can be a simple e-mail survey, asking such questions as what do we do well? And what can we improve? Or simply pick up the phone or go and see them and ask the same questions.

3. Review any complaints or comments – don't just look at those your business gets directly, but check out social media such as Twitter to see what people are saying about your business.

4. So, before you start delivering great customer service, take a moment to think about how you get customer feedback!

How can a customer give you feedback – how easy is it and how do you ask for it?	
What do you do with it – what plans do you have to improve your business and how do you use customer feedback?	
How often do you make a change based on customer feedback?	
Do you thank customers for feedback and tell them what you will do with it? How?	
Do you tell customers about the changes and why you changed? How?	

Finally – go through the feedback and mark on the map where customer issues are. Then you can put together a plan to fix them. Don't forget to thank customers for their feedback and tell them about the changes – otherwise they will think you weren't listening and don't really care what they think!

What are the different journeys a customer could take through your business – initial enquiry, buying, asking for information, upgrading, querying a bill, complaining, leaving?	
Do you know what all the different touch points are and how they link together?	
Do you know what customers like and don't like about each aspect of doing business with you?	

Chapter 5

The 6 things that all customers want: make it easy

Over the last 30 years I've spoken to thousands of customers, read lots of surveys and research and analysed tens of thousands of complaints and comments. It may be just that I'm a very simple person, but I believe it all comes down to there being 6 things that all customers want and that delivering those is the key to great customer service.

When you read them, you'll see they are all just common sense – but it's very easy to get them wrong, even in a small way – and it's the things that seem small to a business that normally end up irritating and confusing customers!

The first thing customers want is MAKE IT EASY.

Sounds obvious doesn't it? – we all want an easy life, we're all customers and it should be easy to do business with a company!

Making it easy to do business with you is very simple – just think of what you want the customer to do, then make sure they can do it as quickly as possible in a way that is obvious to them. When thinking about what you want the customer to do, it's normally things like:

- Understand how my business can help them
- Get all the information they need to make a decision or answer a query
- Buy your product or service
- Understand how to use it
- Know how long something will take

For example, a football club asked me to help because they weren't getting any enquiries about advertising boards through their website. When I mapped the customer journey, you had to click through 5 different pages just to get a phone number, and there was no information about costs or what was available unless you phoned. It was just too much effort for a potential customer. We redesigned the journey – changed the homepage so it was obvious which link to click and the next page gave full details of what was available, the costs and included an online order or query form, with a phone number if the customer needed more detail. Enquiries increased dramatically.

It's not just about websites – how many times have you gone into a shop and had to wander around looking for what you want because there are no clear signs? One of my pet hates is cafes and restaurants where it's not obvious if they bring the bill to you or if you have to go to the till to pay. It might be a small thing, but it can be really frustrating waiting to get the waiter's attention to ask for the bill only to be told to go to the till and pay! Another part of Make It Easy is the amount of choice you give a customer. Many businesses pride themselves on having lots of products and services available, but this can be confusing for customers, especially if they don't know what they want, just what problem or issue they want to solve.

For example, I did some work for a gas and electricity company who had 30 different versions of their products or tariffs and presented them to customers as a long list. They couldn't understand why customers found it hard to pick one. We found it was because customers wanted to know which was the right one for them, and that the list just wasn't helping so they gave up.

We designed a simple questionnaire for customers which took them less than a minute to complete and then showed them no more than 3 products to consider, with an explanation of why they were the right ones for them. It's the same for most businesses – customers want to buy a product or service once they know how they will benefit, so sometimes you need to ask some questions and help guide the customer to the right product for them.

Think about your staff as well – how easy is it for them to serve your customers? Do they have all the tools they need to answer any customer query? Is it all in one place or do they have to go and look for it – taking longer to serve the customer and being less efficient for your business?

Checklist to Make It Easy

What do you want the customer to do?	How many steps do they have to take to do it?	How obvious is each step?	Is it obvious how they benefit (is guidance needed?)

Chapter 6

The 6 things that all customers want: set my expectations

As a customer, I want to know what's going to happen as well as when and how. Open, honest communication is key to developing a good relationship with your customers and also saves you money as it increases sales whilst cutting down on queries and complaints.
For example:

- When you promote your products or services, make sure you explain exactly what the customer gets, when they will get it, how they can use it and how to get help or information if they need it.
- When a customer orders something from you, tell them when and how it will be sent and include a way to contact you if it doesn't arrive on time.
- If a customer complains and you can't resolve it immediately, tell them when you will have an answer, how you will contact them and who is looking into it for them.
- If you promise to do something for the customer, make sure you can do it by that time!

Take time to think about what a customer should expect – again you need to try and think as a customer. This can be difficult (most companies get it wrong – remember 80% of businesses think they deliver great service but only 8% of customers agree!) especially when you know so much more about your products and services than a customer ever will, but it's well worth doing. One way I've seen work really well is to have an empty chair in the room with you – just put a sheet of paper on it with "customer" written on it. It's surprising how something as simple as that makes you stop and ask, "what would the customer expect?"
It's really important not to over promise – many companies do this but it always leads to customer queries as they feel they have been let down. Make sure your staff who deal with customers know how long something WILL take, not how long it SHOULD take. I worked with a company whose customers could upgrade their product online. When they did so, they got a message saying that they had been upgraded – but the company needed

to make some manual changes to deliver the upgrade and they were 6 months behind so the upgrade hadn't actually happened. The next time the customer got a bill, they phoned and complained. Even worse, the call centre staff were told to tell the customer it would be sorted out in 7 days, even though it wouldn't be – so the customers called multiple times chasing the upgrade, creating angry customers who started to leave, and lots of cost for the company.

I'm old enough to remember the adverts for Ronseal – "it does what it says on the tin", and I believe that's how a business should behave. Don't attract customers by promising the earth when you can't deliver it – you may have lots of sales initially but you won't get any repeat business!

A checklist for setting customer expectations:

What is the customer doing?	What do they need to know?	Are we telling them accurately?	How are we telling them?	How can they get help if needed?

Chapter 7

The 6 things that all customers want: keep your promises

Always remember that you have a relationship with your customer – and that relationships are based on trust. It can take people a while to build up trust, and it normally happens because they see that you keep your promises. On the flip side, you can destroy trust very quickly if you break a promise and it can take a long time to rebuild the relationship. On average, it will take 12 positive experiences (or kept promises) before a customer will forgive you for one broken promise!

I'm not daft enough to believe that you can keep every promise in the real world, especially in business. Things go wrong, third parties can let you down and something can take you longer than you thought, so there is one important promise that you must make to all customers, which is that you will tell them if something doesn't happen when or how you said it would, and that you will fix it. I explain more about this in Chapter 10.

So, the first thing to do is to list all the promises you make to your customers. Although this sounds easy, you do need to think long and hard about this.

Why? Well, there are 2 types of promises. Listing the first type is easy – these are explicit promises. For example:

- We will send your product by post the same day if you order before 2pm Monday to Friday, or the next working day if you order after 2pm
- We are open 9am to 5pm Monday to Friday, closed weekends and bank holidays
- We will answer your query within 24 hours

The second type of promise is implicit rather than explicit. This means that, although you may not think you are making a promise, the customer may think you are because of what you say, how you say it or what you do.

Listing these types of promises means you have to look at every aspect of your business and try to think as a customer – "if I say, do or write this, what will a customer then expect?"

For example, John Lewis advertise themselves as being "never knowingly undersold": That's different from saying "we are always the cheapest", but there is an implied promise that they will monitor competitors' prices and beat or match them. John Lewis realise this, so they have a price guarantee which backs it up and gives their customers confidence that they don't need to shop around.

Another example is promoting a "quality" service. To a customer this could mean many things – friendly, attentive, expert staff, personal service, instant answers to queries and so on. Think about what you mean by quality before you tell customers about it!

As a final example suppose your business offers a product that you have to install and then train someone in how to use it. You could say, "Our experts will install the product, make sure it is fully working, and then train your staff how to use it." By that, you may mean you will do a half hour training session with the staff that are there when it is installed. The customer may think, however, that you offer ongoing training, so when they get new staff you will come along and train them as well. See what I mean? It's really important that any promises you make, whether explicit or implied, are clear to the customer – especially when there are limits to what you will do.

When you've listed all your promises, have a coffee!

Next you need to think about what processes you have in place to keep those promises. Take the example of installing a product and training staff: in this case, the business has employed a fitter who will install the product and conduct the initial training – but to make a profit, they need the fitter to be doing this every day, so they can't afford for the fitter to be going back to existing customers just to train more staff. In this case, the promise would be changed to "our experts will install the product and train your staff on the day we install. We'll give you a guide and you can phone us if you need any further support". By changing the promise, the business has made it very clear to the customer what they are getting for their money, but it now needs to make sure that it has a guide available and that there is someone available by phone to answer customer queries.

And it's the same for each of the promises you make – make sure you really understand what the customer would expect, then make sure you have the processes in place. If you don't, then you need to decide whether to change the promise or change your processes!

A checklist for customer promises:

What is the promise?	What will the customer expect?	Have we the processes in place to deliver this?	If no, do we change the promise or the process?	Details of the new promise or process

Chapter 8

The 6 things that all customers want: keep me informed

Keeping customers informed is relatively straightforward (well, it's easier than listing all your promises anyway!).

First you need to think about what information the customer would want at each touchpoint with your business.

For someone becoming aware of your business, it's "what do you do", how can it benefit me", how much does it cost", "how do I find out more".

For someone considering using your products or services it's "how can it benefit me", "how much does it cost", how long will it take", "what do you do to help me".

For someone using your services, it's "how do I use it", "what if something goes wrong", "what do I need to do", "what will happen, when and how", "what of something changes".

For someone stopping doing business with you, it's "how do I tell you", "what will you do", how long will it take", how much will I have to pay/get back".

The question "how will it benefit me" is really important. Customers don't want to know all about the features of a product, they just want to know what it will do for them. For example, you might describe a washing machine as having a new improved motor with an integrated circuit board – what the customer wants to know is that it uses 35% less energy than other washing machines so is cheaper to run, saving them money!

When you have listed all the information a customer could want at each touch point, check to make sure they have easy access to it. Ideally this would mean they can see everything they want to immediately or, at worst, that they would only have to do one thing to get the information – for example, click onto another webpage or phone you.

If a customer has a query and you have to get back to them with an answer, make sure you tell them how long it will take you and how you will get the information to them – this sets their expectations so they are happy, and saves you time and money in the long run as you don't have to keep answering the phone when they chase you for the information!

The other part of keeping customers informed is telling them about other products or services that may be of interest to them. It's important not to bombard them with lots of information about things they wouldn't be interested in though!

Amazon have got this right in one way – when you buy books through their website they show you a list of other authors and books that you may be interested in. I've spent £000's with them over the years because of this! They haven't got it right in other ways though – I only get this information when I log onto their website so they are reactive rather than proactive. If they were proactive, they would e-mail me when one of my favourite authors has a new book out, with a link to their site so I could buy it!

So, keeping customers informed is partly about getting the basic information they will need available when they need it, but, to really build your business, it's about understanding your customer and their needs and proactively communicating to them when you have a new product or service that they would want or would benefit from.

I did some work for a broadband and phone consultant recently. They were really good at giving new customers all the information and training they needed and couldn't understand why they were losing so many customers at the end of their contract. It was simply down to poor communication during the contract – they didn't contact the customer until 18 months after the installation, and then it was just to ask if everything was OK and if the contract would be renewed. When I spoke to the customers, they expected the consultant to regularly check that they were still on the right contract based on their usage, and to recommend changes when necessary that would save the customer money. The changes would have also meant a new 2 year contract being signed so the business wouldn't have lost the customer! Good communication is vital to build a great relationship with your customer and will pay you back multiple times as customers will buy more, stay longer and refer others to you!

Checklist for basic communication:

Which touch point is it?	What will the customer want to know?	Is all the information there?	If no, can the customer get it by doing one more thing?

Checklist for proactive communication:

What needs does the customer have?	Do they have the need now or in the future?	Are we sending them the information when they need it (and explaining the benefits to them)?	Are we sending only relevant information?

Chapter 9

The 6 things that all customers want: treat me as an individual

OK, I've worked with all sizes of businesses, and I know that, the larger the business becomes, the more important it is to have efficient processes in place that are the same for most or every customer, and that it's almost impossible to treat every customer differently. But that's not the point of this – you don't need to treat every customer differently to make them feel you are treating them as an individual – after all, they don't know how you treat everyone else!

This is about knowing your customer, keeping relevant information on them and using it when you communicate with them.

For example, I used to stop regularly at a family run pub in the Midlands. I phoned them recently to book a room for one night, having not stopped there for more than 9 months. The lady who answered the phone explained that their computer was down so took my name and number and promised to call me back. When she did, she said she had booked me a room "I've booked number 3 for you as we know that was your favourite room", that they were looking forward to seeing me again and that they would make sure they had a bottle of my favourite wine in stock! Great service that made me feel really special – yet very simple for them to deliver as they had simply kept detailed notes of my previous stays and preferences!

Loyalty cards are a great way to treat customers as individuals – the likes of Tesco have had them for years, but there are versions you can get for smaller businesses which work just as well. The advantage for the customer is that they get rewarded for their loyalty and feel that their business is appreciated. The advantage for the business is that you get lots of information about the customer and can use that for carefully targeted, relevant communications that will generate higher sales.

There are some simple ways to make sure your customers feel you treat them as individuals:

1. Train your staff to use the customer's name – especially on the phone. The best way to answer the phone is: "Thank you for calling [business name], my name is xxxx, how can I help you"?

Listen to what the customer says and make sure you ask for and then use their name.

2. Keep accurate up to date records of all customer interactions, especially purchases and queries or complaints. More importantly, keep them all in one place where your staff can access and update them quickly. That way, whenever they are talking to customers, they can refer back to previous conversations or purchases so the customer feels that they know them.

3. Train your staff in empathy skills. For example, many businesses don't want their staff to immediately apologise when a customer makes a complaint as they feel that is accepting responsibility, but it's actually more important to the customer that you show empathy by saying something such as, "I'm sorry you have had to complain and I'll do everything I can to help you." It shows that you are aware of how the customer feels!

4. When you have consistent business processes that apply to every customer, train your staff to explain them in a way that is specific to the customer. For example, rather than saying "what we do is...." They should be saying "what I can do for you is.... See the difference?

5. Use the information you hold about the customer to send them information about new products and services that they should be interested in – don't bombard them with irrelevant information!

6. Use the customer name when you send e-mails or mailshots.

7. When you collect information about the customer, look to find out when they are likely to need a product or service from you again. If you sell a contract that is renewed regularly such as car insurance, it's easy to know when to contact the customer again but, if for example you sell paint and wallpaper, make a note of which room(s) they are decorating and ask what their future plans are – so you can contact them when you know they are planning to decorate again.

Checklist for treating me as an individual:

	Staff training	Customer records	Communications
Use of customer name			
All relevant information used			
Customer needs identified			
Does this show empathy – if so, how?			

Chapter 10

The 6 things that all customers want: put it right if it goes wrong!

No business is perfect – systems break down, people make mistakes, suppliers let you down, work can take longer than expected, circumstances can change and the weather can get in the way sometimes as well!

If you've mapped out your customer journeys, made sure you are easy to do business with by reviewing your customer touch points, checked that you are setting customer expectations properly, that you can meet them in normal circumstances, and that you are communicating what the customer needs to know when and how they want it, then it should just be something unexpected that causes a problem.

And if a problem does come up, you are going to find out about it one of two ways – either someone in the business will find out about it before any customer does, or a customer is going to tell you!

It's obviously better if you find out about a problem before the customer, because then you are in control and can quickly put plans in place to sort it out. So how do you do that?

First, it's really important to have a set of internal service standards (also known as service level agreements), and that all your staff know about the ones that are relevant to them, and the impact that missing a standard can have – on the other areas of the business and the customer. Large businesses often have a number of separate departments which can operate in silos – focused on their own work and not really aware of the impact they have on other departments and ultimately the customer. Clear service standards get rid of that problem.

It's just as important to have agreed service standards with all your suppliers as well – and they should all fit together so you can control the service you offer to your customers.

I know it sounds complicated, so here's an example!

Say I run Company A, which buys product kits from Company B, puts the product together, sells it to customers and employs Company C to install them.

I have a service level agreement with Company B which says they will deliver the kit 2 working days from the order being placed and that they will replace any broken or missing parts within 1 day of being notified. The agreement also says they will tell me immediately if they cannot deliver in the agreed time.

I have an internal service level agreement with my engineering department that they will check the kit for broken or missing parts and build the product within 3 days of the kit being received and that they will add missing or change broken parts the same day that they are received. The agreement also says that they will tell me immediately if a job cannot be completed in the agreed time.

I have a service level agreement with Company C which says they will install the product on a date I give them provided they have at least 5 days notice, and that they will tell me immediately if they cannot install when agreed.

So what does all that mean? – well, I know that I can have a full kit delivered within 5 days, build the product within 4 days and have it installed within 5 days so I can sell the product to a customer and promise to have it installed 2 weeks after they have ordered. I've clearly set the customer expectations.

The second element that is really important is what processes you have in place to put something right when you know it has gone wrong. In the above example, because the agreements say that I will be told immediately there are any delays, I can work out if the delay will impact the installation and can proactively contact the customer to explain and rearrange installation.

So what do you do if a customer tells you about a problem you didn't know about?

First – don't tell them that you know about the problem. I've often listened to call centre staff who have taken a complaint call from a customer, have told the customer that the company is aware of the problem and then explained what will happen – it's really annoying to be told that as a customer. If you knew about the problem then why didn't you tell me! Recently I found that I couldn't send or receive e-mails and spent 2 hours trying to find out what the problem was, trying different ways to fix it until I finally phoned the company who run my server – only to be told, "Oh yes, we know about that, we moved some files and corrupted the system – we're working on it now and it should be up and running in the next few hours – just keep trying!" It's not a huge company, not many customers were affected so they could (and should) have picked up the phone! – I'm looking for a new provider now!

Apologise to the customer that they have had to complain, tell them you will look into it and agree when and how you will come back to them (unless you can make immediate enquiries and sort it out on that call, which is always the best way!)

Look into how the problem happened, get the right solution for the customer and make sure they are happy. Next, check if any other customers are impacted – if so, tell them! Then you need to make sure it doesn't happen again – put a permanent solution in place. Don't make the mistake of putting a "work round" or temporary fix in place – I've seen lots of businesses do that and then they never deliver the permanent solution because it's no longer a priority for them. This always adds extra cost to the business and often creates other problems somewhere else!

As an example, let's go back to Company A – a customer calls to say that the engineer hasn't turned up when promised to install the product. When I check with the installer, they tell me that when they called to pick up the product it wasn't ready so the problem is with the engineering department. They tell me that 2 people were off sick so it was taking them 2 extra days to build the product – and that no-one had told me because the manager was off sick and they hadn't told the rest of the department what the service standard was.

So, the first thing I need to do is contact the customer, apologise and explain and set a new installation date. Then I need to check that any other customers who may be impacted are told and finally make sure that everyone knows what the service standards are and why they are important!

To summarise:

- Have service standards both in your company and with suppliers and other third parties

- Review the service standards to make sure they all fit together and support the promises you make to customers

- Make sure everyone in your company knows what the service standards are and the impact on other teams and the customer if they do not meet them

- Ensure that part of each service standard is to let you know immediately they cannot make the standard

- Have a process in place to understand how not hitting a standard will impact the customer, which customers will be impacted and how you will communicate with them

- Have a process in place to investigate the root cause of every customer complaint and correct it

- Have a process in place to tell customers about changes you make so they can see that you are responding to their problems

Checklist for put it right:

Product or service	Internal service standards in place?	External service standards in place?	Back up plan in place?

Chapter 11

The mistakes to avoid

These are the mistakes I've seen companies large and small make in the last 30 years. Although I can't guarantee you will have more customers buying more for longer and referring others to you by following the advice in this book, I haven't yet seen a business fail to improve its results by doing so. I have seen businesses lose sales, customers and profits by making one or more of these mistakes:

1. **Not looking for customer feedback** – I've worked with many small business owners, most of whom have been great salespeople who have been successful working for a large company then gone into business for themselves thinking it's all about sales. It's not! Successful businesses build relationships with their customers through customer feedback.

2. **Not doing anything with customer feedback** – please don't do this half-heartedly. Customer feedback is a valuable tool to use in building a business – BUT YOU HAVE TO USE IT! When you ask for feedback, customers at first appreciate it because they think you value their opinions and are listening to them. If you don't use it then they realise you aren't really listening to them and aren't interested in them so they stop using you!

3. **Not telling the customer when they have made changes** – if you don't show the customer that you have listened to them and made changes you may as well have not bothered to make the changes! They may not see a change for a while through dealing with you in the normal way of business and then may not realise its due to customer feedback, so tell them when you have made changes and why! – it's a great message to customers – because we care about you, we listen to you and we change our business when you tell us changes need to be made!

4. **Bundling a number of small changes into a large project**. I've seen many businesses do this, especially large ones. They wait until they have a large number of changes, create a project, work out what resource and budget they need and go to the board for approval. One of two things happens – either the board rejects the plan because they want to spend the budget on something else that they think is more exciting, or they start to question lots of the changes and the way the project is put together and it takes months of effort to get started, if indeed it ever starts!

5. **Comparing themselves with competitors rather than learning from customers** – your customers deal with you, not your competitors. If you start to copy what they do you will just be a pale imitation of them and you won't be sure you are delivering what your customers want. Focus on your customers and the competitors will soon start watching you!

6. **Stopping making changes when they've hit their target**. I worked with a business that wanted to be ranked as #1 in customer experience amongst its direct competitors. They spent 2 years trying to get there, managed to get to #1 so stopped making changes. The next time the survey came out they were #5 – because their competitors were continually improving. IF YOU STOP MAKING CHANGES YOU DON'T STAND STILL – YOU GO BACKWARDS! It's even harder to start again so just keep going making regular change. It becomes a habit!

7. **Not involving staff in making changes**. I've seen many small business owners become very protective about their business (I've done it myself!), having to have the final say on everything and thinking that only their ideas would work (yes, I've done that as well!). The changes that have the most impact are those that deal with issues highlighted by customer feedback, with solutions designed and delivered with staff – especially those who deal with customers every day. Not only do you get the best solutions, your staff are bought into them from the start so you never need to explain why you are changing!

8. **Not bothering with small changes**. Often businesses focus on big change. The problem is that it's normally the small things that irritate customers most! Remember the quote from Maya Angelou - "people will forget what you said, people will forget what you did, but people will never forget how you made them feel". It's the small things that make people remember how you made them feel – "they didn't phone me when they promised", "they never reply to e-mails", "I had to explain my problem every time I phoned" and so on!

Chapter 12

Checklists for great customer service:

1 Describe your business as a friend:

My business is a:	

It behaves like this:	

2 Who are your customers anyway?

What do you say about your business to prospective customers – what promises are you making and are you confident you can keep them?	
How easy is it for existing customers to contact you – what channels do they want to use?	

How do you treat customers who decide to leave? How do you keep in touch with them?	
What do you do to get feedback and ideas from your staff? How do you involve them in designing and delivering changes to the business?	

3 Customer feedback and journeys

How can a customer give you feedback – how easy is it and how do you ask for it?	
What do you do with it – what plans do you have to improve your business and how do you use customer feedback?	
How often do you make a change based on customer feedback?	

Do you thank customers for feedback and tell them what you will do with it? How?	
Do you tell customers about the changes and why you changed? How?	

What are the different journeys a customer could take through your business – initial enquiry, buying, asking for information, upgrading, querying a bill, complaining, leaving?	

Do you know what all the different touch points are and how they link together?	
Do you know what customers like and don't like about each aspect of doing business with you?	

4 Make it easy:

What do you want the customer to do?	How many steps do they have to take to do it?	How obvious is each step?	Is it obvious how they benefit (is guidance needed?)

5 Setting customer expectations

What is the customer doing?	What do they need to know?	Are we telling them accurately?	How are we telling them?	How can they get help if needed?

7 Keeping your promises

What is the promise?	What will the customer expect?	Have we the processes in place to deliver this?	If no, do we change the promise or the process?	Details of the new promise or process

8 Basic communication

Which touch point is it?	What will the customer want to know?	Is all the information there?	If no, can the customer get it by doing one more thing? (if not, change it!

9 Proactive communication

What needs does the customer have?	Do they have the need now or in the future?	Are we sending them the information when they need it (and explaining the benefits to them)?	Are we sending only relevant information?

10 Treat me as an individual:

	Staff training	Customer records	Communications
Use of customer name			
All relevant information used			
Customer needs identified			

Does this show empathy – if so, how?			

11 Put it right:

Product or service	Internal service standards in place?	External service standards in place?	Back up plan in place?

BITE-SIZED
BOOKS

The most successful people all share an ability to focus on what really matters, keeping things understandable and simple. MBAs, metrics and methodologies have their place, but when we are faced with a new business challenge most of us need quick guidance on what matters most, from people who have been there before and who can show us where to start. As Stephen Covey famously said, "The main thing is to keep the main thing, the main thing".

But what exactly is the main thing?

We created Bite-Sized books to help answer precisely that question crisply and quickly, working with writers who are experienced, successful and, of course, engaging to read.

The brief? Distil the *main things* into a book that can be read by an intelligent non-expert comfortably in around 60 minutes. Make sure the book provides the reader with specific tools, ideas and plenty of examples drawn from real life and business. Be a virtual mentor.

Bite-Sized Books don't cover every eventuality, but they are written from the heart by successful people who are happy to share their experience with you and give you the benefit of their success.

Printed in Great Britain
by Amazon

62216334R00037